MARCEL PROUST

REMEMBRANCE OF THINGS PAST
PART TWO: WITHIN A BUDDING GROVE
VOLUME TWO

Adaptation:
Stéphane Heuet • Stanislas Brézet

Art and Color:
Stéphane Heuet

Acknowledgments

Mme. Nicole Dauxin
The Cercle Litteraire Proustien of Cabourg-Balbec
its president Dr. Jean-Paul Henriet
and the members of the jury 2001:
Messieurs Ghislain de Diesbach, Jerome Clement, Gonzague Saint Bris and pro-
fessor Edouard Zarifian,
Mr. Henri Loyette, Head Curator & Director of the Orsay Museum,
Miss Isabelle Cahn, document-keeper, Orsay Museum,
Mr. Diagna N'Daye,
Mr. Jan, Head of the Municipal Archives of the city of Honfleur (Calvados),
Mr. Didier Finkel, Le Home (Calvados)
Mr. Jacques Porcq, mayor of Cabourg (Calvados), Mme. Catherine Sicard-
Martin, Mr. Blenet and the personnel of the Grand Hotel of Cabourg.
Misses Sandrine Bosman and Marielle Pietri, Florentine, Messieurs Gerard
Prosper and Anthony Folliau.

Already available:
Remembrance of Things Past, Part One: Combray, $19.95 hc, $13.95 pb
Part Two: Within a Budding Grove, vol.1, $16.95 hc, $10.95 pb

We have over 150 titles, write for our color catalog:
NBM, 555 8th Ave., Suite 1202, New York, NY 10018
see our website at www.nbmpublishing.com

ISBN 1-56163-342-9 hc., ISBN 1-56163-348-8 pb
© 2002 Guy Delcourt Productions
© 2003 NBM for the English translation
Translated by Joe Johnson
Lettering by Ortho
Printed in Hong Kong

3   2   1

Library of Congress Cataloging-in-Publication Data

Heuet, Stephane.
    [A la recherche du temps perdu. A l'ombre des jeunes filles en fleurs. English]
    Remembrance of things past. In a budding Grove / Marcel Proust ; adaptation by
Stephane Heuet & Stanislas Brezet ; art by Stephane Heuet.
    p.; cm.
    ISBN 1-56163-342-9 (cloth) --ISBN 1-56163-348-8 (pbk.)
    Volume 2
    I. Title: Marcel Proust, Remembrance of things past. II. Title: In a budding Grove. III.
Brezet, Stanislas. IV. Proust, Marcel, 1871-1922. A la recherche du temps perdu. V.
Title.

PN6747.H48 R4513 2002
741.5944--dc21
                                                                          2002019709

Comicslit is an imprint
and trademark of

NANTIER · BEALL · MINOUSTCHINE
Publishing inc.
new york

WITHIN A BUDDING GROVE

VOLUME 2

SHE'S A FRIEND OF THE YOUNG SIMONET GIRL.

I went back because I was to go dine at Rivebelle with Robert and because my grandmother would insist that I lie down for an hour on such evenings before I could leave.

With neither the shyness nor sadness of the evening of my arrival...

...I rang for the attendant who no longer remained silent while I rose along with him in the elevator as in a mobile, thoracic cage displacing itself the length of the ascending column.

At each floor, a golden glimmer reflecting on the rug bespoke the sunset and the lavatory windows.

DO YOU KNOW ANY SIMONET HERE IN BALBEC?

IT SURE SEEMS LIKE I'VE HEARD THAT NAME BEFORE.

HAVE THE LATEST GUEST LIST BROUGHT TO ME.

Since then I've often sought to recall how that name Simonet had sounded to me on the beach. I don't know why I told myself from the very first that the name Simonet had to be that of one of the young ladies.

I entered my room.

As the season advanced, the scene I saw from my window changed.

As if I were seated on a bunk of one of the ships I saw quite near to me, on all sides I was surrounded by images of the sea.

It was without sadness and without regret for it that I let die atop the curtains the hour upon which I ordinarily was seated at the table. For I knew that this day was of a different sort than the others.

I knew that from the chrysalis of this dusk, by a radiant metamorphosis, the gleaming light of the Rivebelle restaurant was preparing to arise.

IT'S TIME.

KNOCK KNOCK

IT'S AIMÉ, SIR.

I'VE BROUGHT THE GUEST LIST.

Before leaving, Aimé just had to tell me that Dreyfus was guilty a thousand times over.

WE'LL KNOW EVERYTHING, MAYBE NOT THIS YEAR, BUT NEXT; A GENTLEMAN WITH GOOD CONNECTIONS AT HEADQUARTERS TOLD ME SO.

YOU DON'T SUPPOSE THEY'LL DECIDE TO REVEAL EVERYTHING RIGHT AWAY?

It wasn't without a slight pang to my heart that, on the first page of the guest list, I espied the words: "Simonet and family".

We left to dine at Rivebelle.

WON'T YOU BE COLD?
MAYBE YOU'D BETTER KEEP
IT; IT'S NOT VERY WARM.

NO, NO.

From that moment on, I was a new man, who was no longer my grandmother's grandson and would only remember her upon leaving, but was the temporary brother of the waiters who were going to serve us.

I gave the violinist who'd just played the two gold Louis I'd been saving for a month planning some purchase I'd forgotten.

I looked at the round tables whose innumerable assemblage filled the restaurant, like so many planets, just like those that are pictured in the allegorical paintings of yesteryear.

And I felt a little pity for all the diners because I sensed that, for them, the round tables weren't planets and that they hadn't taken a wider view of things which sheds for us their customary appearance and allows us to perceive analogies.

IT'S YOUNG SAINT-LOUP. IT SEEMS HE'S STILL TAKEN WITH HIS CALL GIRL. QUITE THE LOVE THERE.

WHAT A PRETTY FELLOW!

HUSH NOW, HE'S SEEN ME, HE'S LAUGHING, OH! HE KNEW ME WELL.

I GOT TO KNOW HIM WHEN I WAS SEEING D'ORLEANS.

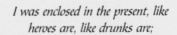

I'd have liked for him to introduce me to these women, liked to be able to ask them for a rendezvous and that they'd grant me one, even if I couldn't have accepted.

If by chance he finished off the evening with some band of his friends...

GO ON WITHOUT ME, WE'RE OFF TO LOSE SOME MONEY AT THE CASINO.

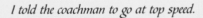
I told the coachman to go at top speed.

By a contradiction that was only apparent, it was at the very moment when I experienced an exceptional pleasure, when I felt that my life could be happy, that without hesitation I would risk it to a chance accident.

I was enclosed in the present, like heroes are, like drunks are;

momentarily eclipsed, my past no longer projected before me that shadow of itself that we call our future.

I was falling into that heavy slumber where are unveiled to us the return to days of youth, the finding of past years, of lost feelings, the disembodiment, the transmigration of souls, the evocation of the dead, the illusions of folly, the regression towards the most elementary realms of nature.

HE DRANK TOO MUCH PORT.

TWO O'CLOCK!

It was a difficult landing...

MESSRS. LEGRANDIN AND CAMBREMER ARE BROTHERS-IN-LAW, AREN'T THEY?

9

aint-Loup's visit soon drew to a close. I'd not seen the girls on the beach again. He stayed at Balbec too short a time in the afternoon to be able to trouble with them and attempt, for my sake, to make their acquaintance. In the evenings, he was freer and continued to take me often to Rivebelle.

WHO'S THAT MAN DINING ALONE? HE ALWAYS ARRIVES AS EVERYONE STARTS LEAVING.

COME NOW, YOU DON'T KNOW THE FAMOUS PAINTER ELSTIR? HE DID THE PAINTING OF THE CROSS AT THE ENTRANCE TO RIVEBELLE. THAT VERY ONE! ALL FOUR PIECES! YES! HE DOES GO TO A LOT OF TROUBLE!

HE'S A FRIEND OF SWANN'S AND A WELL-KNOWN ARTIST, OF GREAT TALENT.

We wrote a letter signed with our names.

He'd been one of the first to frequent this restaurant back when it was only still a farm of sorts and to bring a colony of artists there (who had, moreover, all moved along elsewhere once the farm, where people had eaten outdoors under a simple overhang, had become a fashionable locale; Elstir himself had only returned to Rivebelle at the moment because his wife, with whom he lived not far away, was away).

HE GAVE ME A SUNRISE OVER THE SEA. IT MUST BE WORTH A FORTUNE, NO?

Our enthusiasm for Elstir was not, as we reckoned it, out of admiration, since we'd never seen anything by Elstir. It was at best empty admiration.

Due to a lack of tolerable society, he lived in such isolation, so unsociably, that worldly folk called it posturing and poor education, officials bad disposition, his neighbors craziness, his family selfishness and pride.

In the few words that Elstir came to say to us while sitting down at our table, he never answered me the several times when I spoke to him of Swann. I began to think that he didn't know him. He did nonetheless ask me to come see his studio in Balbec, an invitation he didn't extend to Saint-Loup.

I promised myself to go to his studio within the next two or three days...

but the next day...

While on the previous days I'd mostly dwelt on the tall girl, from that afternoon on, it was the one with the golf clubs, presumably Miss Simonet, who once again began to occupy my thoughts.

But maybe it was rather the one with a complexion of geraniums, with green eyes, that I'd have most liked to meet.

I didn't love one but all of them.

Whomever it was, on a given day, that I preferred to see, the others, though without that one, sufficed to move me; my desire, even if it was sometimes directed towards one, or sometimes directed towards another, continued -like, on the first day, my confused vision- to unite them, to make of them a little world apart animated with a common life which they moreover had, no doubt, the pretension to constitute; I would have entered, by becoming the friend of one of them -like a refined pagan or a scrupulous Christian among barbarians-, a rejuvenating society where there reigned health, unconsciousness, sensuality, cruelty, unintellectuality, and joy.

IT'S ABSURD AND NOT VERY NICE TO NOT GO SEE MONSIEUR ELSTIR.

But I could only think about the little band.

SUCH ELEGANCE! YOU'VE BEEN CHANGING SUITS EVERY DAY...

...I'd even written to Paris to have some new hats and ties sent to me.

I made use of every pretext to go to the beach at times when I hoped to be able to catch them there.

COME NOW, STAY WITH ME A LITTLE WHILE LONGER!

For now, those young girls were making me forget my own grandmother.

I didn't know whether they'd be leaving for America or returning to Paris. That was enough to make me start to fall for them. You can have a liking for someone. But to unleash that sadness, that feeling of the irreparable, those feelings of anguish that prepare the way for love, the risk of impossibility is required.

I ended up having to obey my grandmother, with all the more annoyance since Elstir lived rather far from the beach, in one of Balbec's newest avenues.

Elstir's villa was perhaps the most sumptuously hideous, rented by him despite that, because of all those that there were in Balbec, it was the only one that could provide him with a very big studio.

Elstir's studio seemed to me like the laboratory of a sort of new creation of the world.

Naturally, what he had in his studio was mostly seascapes done here in Balbec. But I could discern in them that the charm of each one consisted in a sort of metamorphosis of the things pictured, analogous to that which, in poetry, is called a metaphor.

One of his most frequent metaphors was indeed one which, comparing the land to the sea, suppresses every demarcation betwixt them.

Perhaps it's for a metaphor of this kind —in a painting representing the port of Carquethuit, a painting he'd only finished a few short days before— that Elstir had prepared the viewer's spirit by employing for the little town only marine terms, and only urban ones for the sea.

The entire painting gave the impression of harbors where the sea enters into the earth, where the land has become wetlands, and its populace amphibian. The force of the marine element was bursting through everywhere.

WHAT? THE CHURCH IN BALBEC?

YOU WERE DISAPPOINTED BY THAT PORCH?

BUT IT'S THE MOST BEAUTIFULLY ORNAMENTED BIBLE THAT THE PEOPLE HAVE EVER HAD TO READ!

THAT VIRGIN AND ALL THE BAS-RELIEFS THAT RECOUNT HER LIFE IS THE SWEETEST, MOST INSPIRED EXPRESSION OF THAT LONG POEM OF ADORATION AND PRAISE THAT THE MIDDLE AGES PROFFERED TO THE GLORY OF THE MADONNA!

THE IDEA OF THAT GREAT VEIL IN WHICH THE ANGELS ARE CARRYING THE BODY OF THE VIRGIN, TOO SACRED FOR THEM TO DARE TOUCH HER DIRECTLY...

AND THE ONE WHO DIPS HIS HAND INTO JESUS' BATH WATER TO SEE IF IT'S HOT ENOUGH...

AND ONE OUT OF THE CLOUDS...

AND ALL THOSE WHO, GAZING OVER THEM FROM HEAVEN ON HIGH...

...IT'S ALL THE CIRCLES OF HEAVEN, THE WHOLE A GIGANTIC, THEOLOGICAL AND SYMBOLIC POEM THAT YOU HAVE THERE. IT'S MAD, IT'S DIVINE, IT'S A THOUSAND TIMES SUPERIOR TO ANYTHING YOU'LL SEE IN ITALY

...WHERE, MOREOVER, THIS TYMPANUM WAS LITERALLY COPIED BY SCULPTORS OF FAR LESS GENIUS.

BECAUSE, YOU UNDERSTAND, IT'S ALL A QUESTION OF GENIUS. THERE'S NEVER BEEN AN ERA WHEN EVERYONE HAD GENIUS, THAT'S JUST LUDICROUS, IT WOULD SURPASS THE GOLDEN AGE.

That vast, celestial vision, that gigantic theological poem that I understood to have been written there, when my eyes, so full of desire, had gazed upon the façade, that wasn't what I'd seen.

I WAS EXPECTING TO FIND AN ALMOST PERSIAN MONUMENT. THAT'S NO DOUBT WHAT DISAPPOINTED ME.

WELL, NO, THERE'S SOMETHING TO THAT.

CERTAIN PARTS ARE VERY ORIENTAL.

ONE CAPITAL REPRODUCES A PERSIAN SUBJECT SO EXACTLY THAT THE PERSISTENCE OF ORIENTAL TRADITIONS DOESN'T SUFFICE TO EXPLAIN IT.

THE SCULPTOR MUST HAVE COPIED SOME CASKET BROUGHT BACK BY EXPLORERS.

?

DO YOU KNOW THAT GIRL, SIR?

Elstir told me that her name was Albertine Simonet and also told me the names of her other friends whom I described to him with sufficient exactitude that he showed scarcely any hesitation.

A DAY DOESN'T GO BY WITHOUT ONE OR MORE OF THEM PASSING BY THE STUDIO AND COMING IN TO PAY ME A SHORT VISIT.

I had committed a social error with respect to their social situation.

I had situated in a suspect milieu the daughters of the very well-off lower bourgeoisie, of the world of industry and business.

If I'd only been to see him as soon as my grandmother had asked me to do so, I'd have probably already long since made Albertine's acquaintance.

I could only admire the extent to which the French bourgeoisie was a marvelous studio for the noblest, most varied sculpture. What unpredictable types, what invention in the character of faces, what decisiveness, what freshness, what simplicity in their features! The stingy old businessmen from whom had sprung these Dianas and nymphs seemed to me the greatest of statuaries.

I thought that she'd gone to rejoin her friends at the waterfront. If I could have been there along with Elstir, I might have made their acquaintance.

I invented a thousand pretexts so that he would agree to come take a stroll with me on the beach.

HAPPILY, BUT I MUST FIRST FINISH THIS BIT.

Thus did I find myself bringing to light a watercolor that must have been from a much earlier time in Elstir's life.

On the bottom of the portrait was written: Miss Sacripant, October 1872. I couldn't hold back my admiration.

OH! IT'S NOTHING, JUST A YOUTHFUL SKETCH, IT WAS AN OUTFIT FOR A VARIETY MAGAZINE. IT'S ALL LONG AGO NOW.

WHAT HAPPENED TO THE MODEL?

QUICK, HAND ME THAT PAINTING, I HEAR MRS. ELSTIR COMING AND, EVEN THOUGH THE YOUNG PERSON WITH THE BOWLER HAT NEVER PLAYED, I ASSURE YOU, ANY PART IN MY LIFE, THERE'S NO POINT IN MY WIFE HAVING TO SEE THAT WATERCOLOR.

I'VE ONLY KEPT IT AS AN AMUSING RECORD OF THE THEATER OF THE TIME.

I REALLY SHOULD JUST KEEP THE HEAD, THE LOWER PART IS REALLY VERY POORLY DONE, THE HANDS ARE THOSE OF A NOVICE.

I regretted Mrs. Elstir's arrival, which would only delay us further.

But she didn't stay very long.

She might have once been beautiful, if she were twenty, herding an ox through the Roman countryside.

MY BEAUTIFUL WIFE.

Later, once I'd become acquainted with Elstir's mythological paintings, Mme. Elstir took on beauty for me, too.

Oh, the ruses I used to get Elstir to remain in the area where I believed the girls might yet pass by! It seemed to me that we'd have more luck locating the small band by going to the end of the beach.

...TELL ME ABOUT CARQUETHUIT.

AH!

...HOW I'D LOVE TO GO TO CARQUETHUIT!...

...without considering that the novel character that manifested itself with such power in the Port of Carquethuit by Elstir, was due perhaps more to the painter's vision than to any special merit of the beach itself.

Night was falling; we had to get back;

Suddenly, like Mephistopheles rising forth in front of Faust...

Feeling that it was inevitable that a meeting between them and us would occur, and that Elstir was going to call me over, I turned my back like a bather who's about to catch a wave. I remained behind, leaning towards an antique dealer's window.

I was considering the display while awaiting the moment when my name being called out by Elstir would come strike me like an expected, inoffensive bullet.

Now that it was inevitable, the pleasure of meeting them became compressed and reduced.

Elstir was going to call me.

?!

It was all a flop.

I WOULD HAVE BEEN SO PLEASED TO MEET THEM.

THEN WHY DID YOU KEEP SO FAR AWAY?

I WAS TELLING YOU ABOUT CARQUETHUIT. I DID A SMALL SKETCH WHERE YOU CAN MUCH BETTER SEE THE CURVATURE OF THE BEACH.

IF YOU WOULD LIKE, AS A TOKEN OF OUR FRIENDSHIP, I'LL GIVE YOU MY SKETCH.

I'D VERY MUCH LIKE TO HAVE A PHOTOGRAPH OF THE SMALL PORTRAIT OF MISS SACRIPANT.

BUT WHAT SORT OF NAME IS THAT?

IT'S A CHARACTER PLAYED BY THE MODEL IN A STUPID, LITTLE OPERETTA.

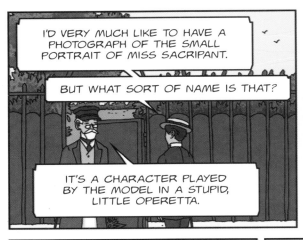

BUT YOU DO REALIZE THAT I DON'T KNOW HER AT ALL, SIR,

YOU SEEM TO THINK OTHERWISE.

BUT ISN'T THAT MADAME SWANN BEFORE HER MARRIAGE?

These sudden, fortuitous stumblings on the truth, which after all are rather rare, suffice, after the fact, to give a certain basis to the theory of premonitions.

Elstir didn't answer me. It really was a portrait of Odette de Crécy. She hadn't wanted to keep it.

Could it be possible that this man of genius was the ridiculous, corrupt painter once "adopted" by the Verdurins?

I asked him if he'd known them, if by chance they hadn't called him "Mr. Biche" back then.

He told me yes, without any embarrassment, as if he didn't suspect the disappointment he was awakening in me; but looking up, he read it on my face.

MONSIEUR BICHE, SINCE YOU WENT TO SEE THAT EXHIBITION, I WOULD LIKE FOR YOU TO TELL ME IF TRULY THERE IS IN THESE LATEST WORKS MORE THAN THAT STUPEFYING VIRTUOSITY...

...I GOT UP CLOSE TO SEE HOW IT WAS DONE, I PUT MY NOSE ON IT. AH! HMMPH!...

THAT BICHE IS SO AMUSING!

...ONE COULDN'T SAY WHETHER IT WAS MADE WITH GLUE, WITH BRONZE, WITH SUNLIGHT, WITH EXCREMENT!...

Rather than words that might have avenged his self-esteem, he preferred those that could instruct me:

THERE IS NO MAN, HOWEVER WISE HE MAY BE, WHO HASN'T AT SOME POINT IN HIS YOUTH, UTTERED WORDS, OR EVEN LED A LIFE WHOSE MEMORY AREN'T UNPLEASANT TO HIM AND THAT HE MIGHT WISH TO ERASE...

...AND IT'S EVEN BETTER A PAW THAN REMBRANDT'S...

...THERE'S NO WAY OF DIS-COVERING HIS TRICK THAN IN DOING THE ROUNDS...

OOOOOH!...

...-IT SMELLS GOOD, IT TAKES YOU OVER, IT CUTS OFF YOUR BREATH, IT TICKLES YOU, AND IT'S IMPOSSIBLE TO KNOW WHAT IT'S MADE OF,

IT'S SORCERY, IT'S TRICKERY, IT'S MIRACULOUS:

IT'S DISHONEST!...

...AND IT'S SO FAITHFUL!

...I KNOW THAT THERE ARE YOUNG PEOPLE TO WHOM THEIR TEACHERS HAVE TAUGHT NOBILITY OF MIND AND MORAL ELEGANCE, BUT THEY'RE POOR SOULS, THE WEAK DESCENDANTS OF DOCTRINAIRES, WHOSE WISDOM IS STERILE.

...YOU DON'T RECEIVE WISDOM, YOU MUST DISCOVER IT YOURSELF.

I left Elstir:

I was disappointed about not having met those young ladies. But at last, now there would be the possibility of meeting them again sometime.

A CARRIAGE OR A TRAIN CAR WILL BE MORE OR LESS THE EQUIVOCABLE.

FINE, I'LL TAKE THE "SLOW POKE" TRAIN.

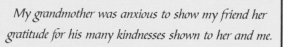

My grandmother was anxious to show my friend her gratitude for his many kindnesses shown to her and me.

YES, THEY'RE LETTERS SIGNED BY PROUDHON.

TAKE THEM WITH YOU, THEY'RE ALL YOURS. I SENT FOR THEM TO GIVE THEM TO YOU.

The next day...

I DIDN'T THANK YOUR GRAND-MOTHER ENOUGH.

I PROMISE TO COME SEE YOU SEVERAL TIMES A WEEK.

YES, YOU COULD COME FOR LUNCH, OR DINNER, OR EVEN A STAY AT DONCIERES.

YOU, TOO, IF EVER YOU SHOULD PASS BY DONCIERES ONE AFTERNOON WHEN I'M FREE, YOU COULD INQUIRE FOR ME IN THE BARRACKS,

BUT I'M HARDLY EVER FREE.

SO WHAT DAY SHALL WE GO?

?

AFTER ALL HIS KINDNESS, IT WOULD BE RUDE OF ME TO NOT ACCEPT HIS INVITATION.

If there wasn't a moment when the young ladies of the small band might be passing by, it was no longer solely towards the sea that I would gaze.

I was attempting to find beauty where I'd never thought it might be, in the most ordinary of things, in the profundity of "still lives."

When, several days after Saint-Loup's departure, I succeeded in getting Elstir to give a small afternoon reception where I would meet Albertine, that charm and elegance that were to be seen in me at the moment I was exiting the hotel, I regretted being unable to reserve for the captivation of some other, more interesting person. My mind judged that to be pleasure of very little worth, now that it was assured.

When I arrived at Elstir's, I thought at first that Miss Simonet wasn't in the studio.

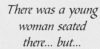

There was a young woman seated there... but...

...I wasn't seeing the entity I'd formed of a young cyclist, wearing a polo cap, strolling along the sea.

Yet it was Albertine.

But even when I realized it, I didn't concern myself with her.

Whenever one participates in any society function,

when you're young,

...you die to yourself, you become like a different man, every room a fresh new universe wherein, swayed by the law of another moral perspective, you focus your attention, as if they might forever matter to us, upon people, dances, card games, that will be forgotten the next day.

COME, SO I CAN INTRODUCE YOU!

I found myself according these sundry events the same importance as my introduction to Miss Simonet.

Which is not to say that the subsequent introduction caused me no pleasure...

Naturally, I didn't realize that pleasure until a little later, when, having returned to the hotel, all alone, I became myself once again. There are pleasures which are like photographs. What you snap in the presence of your beloved is but a negative; you develop it later, once you're home, once you've found at your disposal that dark, inner chamber whose entryway is "condemned" so long as you're surrounded with other people.

At the moment when one's name sounds on the lips of our introducer, especially if he surrounds them, as did Elstir, with flattering comments... that sacramental moment,

analogous to the one in a fairy-tale where the genie orders that a person suddenly become someone else...the one we've been desiring to approach fades away.

As I got closer to the young lady and got to know her better, that acquaintance occurred by way of subtraction. Her name, her connections had been the first limit set to my suppositions. Her kindness was another one. Finally, I was surprised to hear her use the adverb "perfectly" rather than "quite"...

...SHE'S PERFECTLY MAD, BUT VERY SWEET ALL THE SAME...

However unpleasant this use of the word "perfectly" may be, it does indicate a degree of civilization and culture...

...HE'S A PERFECTLY TACKY, AND PERFECTLY BORING, GENTLEMAN...

...to which I couldn't have imagined her attaining, this cycling bacchante, this frenzied muse of golf.

To be finished with that first evening of introductions, while attempting to picture again that small beauty spot over her cheek under her eye, I remembered that, at Elstir's, once Albertine has departed, I'd seen that beauty spot on her chin. In short, when I'd seen her, I noticed that she had a beauty spot, but my errant memory then moved it about Albertine's face, placing it first here then there.

One morning, not long after...

?

WHAT WEATHER! BALBEC'S ENDLESS SUMMER REALLY IS JUST ONE BIG JOKE!

Remembering the "good manners" that had so impressed me, her rude tone and "little band" manners made me feel a converse astonishment.

DON'T YOU EVER DO ANYTHING HERE? WE NEVER SEE YOU PLAYING GOLF OR AT THE CASINO DANCES; YOU DON'T DO ANY HORSEBACK RIDING EITHER. YOU MUST GET PRETTY BORED!

DON'T YOU THINK IT'S DEADLY DULL STAYING ON THE BEACH ALL THE TIME?

AH! BASKING IN THE SUN LIKE A LIZARD IS YOUR THING? ANYHOW YOU'VE GOT LOTS OF TIME. I CAN SEE YOU'RE NOT LIKE ME; I JUST ADORE ALL SPORTS!

YOU DIDN'T GO TO THE SOGNE RACES? WE WENT THERE ON THE TRAM, AND I CAN UNDERSTAND WHY YOU'D NOT HAVE MUCH FUN RIDING SUCH AN OLD WRECK! IT TOOK US TWO HOURS! I COULD'VE GONE THERE AND BACK THREE TIMES ON MY BIKE.

Having admired Saint-Loup when he'd so naturally termed the little local train the "slow poke" because of the endless detours it made, I was intimidated by the facility with which Albertine said words like the "tram" or "wreck."

The beauty spot that I'd remembered being first on her cheek, then on her chin, settled forever on her upper lip, below her nose.

WHY, YOUR FRIENDS WILL BE UNHAPPY IF YOU ABANDON THEM...

OH NO, THEY DON'T NEED ME.

YOU'VE BEEN GOLFING, OCTAVE?

OH! I GOT FED UP WITH IT; MY GAME'S OFF.

WAS ANDREE THERE?

YEAH, SHE SHOT A SEVENTY-SEVEN.

WOW! THAT'S A RECORD!

DO YOU MIND?

With this young man, I was struck by how much the knowledge of everything to do with clothes, how to wear them, cigars, English drinks, and horses had developed in isolation, without being accompanied by the slightest intellectual culture.

HIS FATHER'S A VERY RICH INDUSTRIALIST. HE'S THE HEAD OF THE BALBEC PROPERTY-OWNERS ASSOCIATION.

YOU COULD'VE INTRODUCED ME!

COME ON! I CAN'T INTRODUCE YOU TO A GIGOLO!

THIS PLACE IS FULL OF GIGOLOS. BUT WHAT WOULD THEY SAY TO YOU? HE'S GOT A GOOD GOLF GAME, THAT'S ALL. I KNOW WHAT I'M TALKING ABOUT. HE WOULDN'T BE YOUR SORT AT ALL.

WHO'S THAT BIZARRE CREATURE?

EXCUSE ME, BUT I WANTED TO LET YOU KNOW I'M GOING TO DONCIERES TOMORROW. IT WOULD BE IMPOLITE OF ME TO KEEP ON WAITING, AND I'M WONDERING JUST WHAT SAINT-LOUP-EN-BRAY MUST BE THINKING OF ME.

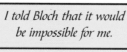

I told Bloch that it would be impossible for me.

OH, WELL THEN, I'LL GO ALONE.

I ADMIT HE'S A HANDSOME ENOUGH FELLOW, BUT HE'S DISGUSTING!

It never occurred to me Bloch might be handsome; he was, in fact.

HE'S MY FRIEND BLOCH.

I'D HAVE BET THAT HE WAS A YID. IT'S JUST LIKE THEM TO BE BUZZING ABOUT.

We parted company, Albertine and I, promising an outing together at some point. I'd chatted with her without being aware of where my words were falling.

I promised myself that, the next time I met Albertine, to be bolder with her, but I said very different things than I'd planned.

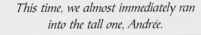

This time, we almost immediately ran into the tall one, Andrée.

Albertine had to introduce me.

Five gentlemen went by whom I'd gotten to know very well by sight since being in Balbec. I'd often wondered who they were.

THEY'RE NOT VERY FASHIONABLE FOLK. THE LITTLE OLD MAN, WITH COLORED HAIR AND YELLOW GLOVES, A FINE TOUCH, EH? HE'S GOT QUITE THE LOOK. HE'S THE BALBEC DENTIST AND A DECENT FELLOW;

THE FAT ONE'S THE MAYOR,

NOT THE SHORT, LITTLE FAT ONE, HE'S THE DANCE TEACHER. HE CAN'T STAND US BECAUSE WE MAKE TOO MUCH NOISE AT THE CASINO.

WITH THEM IS DE SAINTE-CROIX, THE GENERAL COUNCILMAN, WHO'S GONE OVER TO THE REPUBLICANS FOR THE MONEY.

THE SKINNY ONE'S THE ORCHESTRA CONDUCTOR. YOU'VE NOT BEEN TO HEAR CAVALLERIA RUSTICANA? OH! I THINK IT'S WONDER-FUL! HE'S GIVING A CONCERT TONIGHT.

....BUT WE CAN'T GO BECAUSE IT'S TAKING PLACE IN A ROOM IN THE TOWN HALL. IN THE CASINO IT WOULDN'T MATTER, BUT NOT IN A ROOM IN THE TOWN HALL WHERE THEY'VE REMOVED THE CRUCIFIX...

AH! YOU KNOW THE AMBRESAC GIRLS? THEY'RE VERY NICE, BUT SO WELL RAISED THAT THEY'RE NOT ALLOWED TO GO TO THE CASINO.

THEY'RE VERY MUCH THE INNOCENT LITTLE THINGS.

YOU'LL POINT OUT THAT MY AUNT'S HUSBAND IS IN THE GOVERNMENT. BUT WHAT CAN I SAY? MY AUNT'S MY AUNT. THAT'S NOT WHY I LOVE HER! BEING RID OF ME IS THE ONLY THING SHE'S EVER WANTED.

SEEMS THEY DO KNOW HOW TO BE PLEASING, SINCE ONE OF THEM HAS ALREADY GOTTEN ENGAGED TO THE MARQUIS DE SAINT-LOUP.

?!

FOR ME, JUST THEIR WAY OF TALKING GETS ON MY NERVES. AND THEY ALSO DRESS IN A RIDICULOUS MANNER.

NOW, MADAME ELSTIR, THERE'S AN ELEGANT WOMAN.

OH, YEAH? SHE SEEMED TO ME TO BE DRESSED VERY SIMPLY.

SHE DRESSES VERY SIMPLY, IT'S TRUE, BUT SHE DRESSES DELIGHTFULLY.

Albertine felt a great admiration for Elstir himself and was knowledgeable about paintings in a way that very much contrasted with her enthusiasm for Cavalleria Rusticana. Her taste for painting had almost caught up with that for appearance.

I didn't find her to be any more disposed to introducing me to her friends.

YOU'RE VERY KIND TO ATTACH ANY IMPORTANCE TO THEM. DON'T PAY ANY ATTENTION TO THEM, THEY'RE OF NO CONCERN.

ANDREE, AT LEAST, IS REMARKABLY INTELLIGENT. SHE'S A GOOD GIRL, ALTHOUGH PERFECTLY FLIGHTY, BUT THE OTHERS ARE REALLY QUITE STUPID.

I suddenly felt very chagrined that Saint-Loup had concealed his engagement from me, and was doing something as improper as getting married without breaking with his mistress.

One of the following mornings...

HELLO, AM I BOTHERING YOU?

Albertine, irritated perhaps to see her bare-headed, kept a glacial silence despite which the other person remained, kept away from me by Albertine, who arranged at certain moments to be alone with her, at others to be walking with me, leaving the other behind.

So that she'd introduce me, I was obliged to ask Albertine in front of the other girl.

Then I saw a cordial, friendly smile form and gleam.

Catching fire immediately, I told myself that she was a shy child when she was in love

and that it was for me, for love of me, that she'd remained with us.

But the words promised to me by Gisèle's look couldn't be voiced because of Albertine, stubbornly keeping between the two of us, continuing to answer ever more curtly, then ceasing altogether to respond to her friend's questions; the latter ended up leaving.

YOU WERE VERY UNKIND TO HER.

THAT'LL TEACH HER TO BE MORE CIRCUMSPECT!

WHY WAS SHE LATCHING ONTO US?

AND I JUST CAN'T STAND HER WEARING HER HAIR LIKE THAT; IT LOOKS TACKY.

I HADN'T NOTICED.

WELL YOU STARED AT HER LONG ENOUGH; IT LOOKED LIKE YOU WANTED TO DO HER PORTRAIT.

ANYHOW, SHE'LL NO LONGER HAVE THE CHANCE TO BE LATCHING ON AND GETTING DUMPED; SHE'S LEAVING FOR PARIS SOON.

SHE'S GOT TO HIT THE BOOKS, THE POOR THING.

I returned to the hotel, ordered a carriage, and rode to the train station.

Gisèle wouldn't be surprised to see me there.

In the train for Paris, there's a corridor where, while the governess slumbered, I could take Gisèle into dark corners,

plan rendez-vous' with her for my return to Paris, which I would strive to hasten as much as possible.

Still, what would she have thought if she'd known how I'd long hesitated between her and her friends, that just as much as with her, I'd have wanted to be in love with Albertine,

with the young girl with bright eyes, and with Rosemonde!

I felt pangs of remorse,

now that a mutual love was going to unite me with Gisèle.

Several days later, despite the scant enthusiasm Albertine had shown about introducing us, I met all of the little band of that first day, and also two or three girl friends to whom they introduced me when asked.
Soon I spent every day with these girls.

Alas! in the freshest flower, one can discern the imperceptible points that, for the educated mind, already sketch out what will be the immutable and already predestined form of the seed.

It was enough to see by the side of these girls their mother or their aunt, to measure the distances that, under an internal magnetism of a generally horrible kind, those traits would traverse in less than thirty years.

As on a plant where the flowers bloom at different times, I'd seen on this beach in Balbec, those hardened seeds, those flabby tubers as the old ladies my friends would one day be.

But of what importance? For now, it was the season of flowers.

We often ran into Bloch's sisters.

I'M NOT ALLOWED TO PLAY WITH "ISSREALITES."

These young, bourgeois girls from devout families must readily believe that Jews butchered Christian infants.

ALSO, YOUR FRIENDS ARE OF A DIRTY SORT...

....LIKE EVERYTHING TO DO WITH THE TRIBE.

One of their cousins scandalized the Casino for the admiration she showed for Miss Léa,

...whose acting talents the elder Monsieur Bloch highly esteemed, but whose tastes didn't seem directed towards the gentlemen.

Andrée, who'd seemed the coldest to me on the first day, was infinitely more refined, affectionate, and sensitive than Albertine, to whom she showed an elder sister's caressing, sweet affection.

WELL THEN, ANDREE, WHAT ARE YOU WAITING ON? YOU KNOW WE'RE GOING TO PLAY GOLF.

NO, I'M GOING TO STAY AND CHAT WITH HIM.

BUT YOU KNOW MADAME DURIEUX INVITED YOU!

COME ON, MY DEAR, DON'T BE SO STUPID.

DO WHAT YOU LIKE, BUT I'M GONE, CAUSE I THINK YOUR CLOCK'S RUNNING SLOW.

SHE'S A CHARMING GIRL, BUT IMPOSSIBLE.

If, in this taste for amusement, Albertine was something like the Gilberte of previous days, it's because a certain resemblance exists, all the while evolving, between all the women that we love in succession.

Except for rainy days, as we were to go on our bikes to the cliffs or to the countryside, an hour beforehand, I'd try to pretty myself up and would complain if Françoise hadn't prepared my things right.

FRANÇOISE, I CAN'T FIND MY JACKET.

THAT'S BECAUSE I PUT IT AWAY RATHER THAN LETTING IT SIT THERE AND GATHER DUST.

I DON'T UNDERSTAND HOW YOU CAN LEAVE YOUR THINGS ABOUT LIKE THAT

AND YOU TRY AND SEE IF ANYONE ELSE CAN MAKE HEADS OR TAILS OF THIS MESS. THE DEVIL HIMSELF WOULD GET CONFUSED IN HERE.

THIS TRIP TO BALBEC'S HARDLY A VACATION FOR ME!

HERE ARE THE CHEESE AND LETTUCE SAND-WICHES YOU ASKED FOR.

AND DID YOU GET THE PIES?

YES.

YOU KNOW, THEY COULD TAKE TURNS PAYING, TOO, IF THEY WEREN'T SO SELF-INTERESTED.

We took off.

In the past, I'd have preferred our outing to take place in bad weather. Back then I was looking to find in Balbec the "land of the Cimmerians," and sunny days weren't something that ought to have existed there, an intrusion of the vulgar summer of bathers in that ancient region veiled by the mists.

But now everything I disdained, kept from my sight, not only the effects of the sunlight, but even the regattas, the horse races, I sought out passionately.

It's because I sometimes went to see Elstir with my friends

and what he'd preferred to show us were several sketches made of pretty yachting women...

WHAT A TRANSFORMATION OF EVERYTHING IN THAT LUMINOUS VASTNESS OF A RACECOURSE WHERE ONE'S SURPRISED BY SO MANY LIGHTS AND SHADOWS,

WHICH YOU CAN ONLY SEE THERE!

THE FIRST DAY ESPECIALLY WAS EXQUISITE,

or rather a sketch done of a racecourse near Balbec.

....SUCH A LIGHT...AH! I'D HAVE LOVED TO HAVE GOTTEN IT RIGHT;

AND THE REGATTAS!

He waxed even more ecstatic over the yachting events than over the horses,

and I understood that regattas, all sports competitions could, for a modern artist, be a theme as interesting as the festivals a Veronese or a Carpaccio so loved to depict.

YOUR COMPARISON IS ALL THE MORE EXACT BECAUSE OF THE CITY WHERE THEY PAINTED THEM; THOSE PARTIES WERE IN PART ON THE WATER.

THERE WERE WATER COMPETITIONS, JUST LIKE HERE, GENERALLY GIVEN IN HONOR OF SOME EMBASSY, LIKE THE ONE THAT CARPACCIO DEPICTED IN HIS LEGEND OF SAINT URSULA.

I'D REALLY LOVE TO GO TO VENICE!

YOU MAY SOON BE ABLE TO LOOK UPON THE MARVELOUS FABRICS THEY USED TO WEAR THERE.

THEY WERE NO LONGER TO BE SEEN EXCEPT IN THE PICTURES BY VENETIAN PAINTERS.

BUT I'VE HEARD THAT AN ARTIST FROM VENICE, FORTUNY, HAS REDISCOVERED THE SECRET OF MAKING THEM.

I ADMIT TO YOU THAT I PREFER THE STYLES OF TODAY TO THOSE OF VERONESE'S OR EVEN OF CARPACCIO'S TIME.

What's pretty about our yachts is the unified, simple, shining, gray thing that, on cloudy, bluish days, take on a creamy haziness.

Women's outfits on the yachts are the same; what's charming are those light garments, in matching white, made of cloth, linen, nankeen or drill, which in the sunlight and against the blue of the sea shine as dazzling a white as a white sail.

WHILE THERE ARE VERY FEW WOMEN WHO DRESS WELL, SOME HOWEVER ARE MARVELOUS. AT THE RACES, MISS LEA HAD A SMALL, WHITE HAT AND A SMALL, WHITE PARASOL; IT WAS EXQUISITE.

AH, HERE'S SOMEONE WHO'S ALREADY UNDERSTOOD WHAT THE HAT AND PARASOL WERE LIKE.

HOW I'D LOVE TO BE RICH ENOUGH TO HAVE A YACHT! WHAT WONDERFUL TRIPS I'D TAKE!

AND AN AUTOMOBILE!

DO YOU FIND WOMEN'S FASHIONS FOR AUTOMOBILE EXCURSIONS TO BE PRETTY?

NO, BUT THEY WILL BE. MOREOVER, THERE ARE ONLY A FEW REAL FASHION HOUSES, ONE OR TWO, CALLOT, DOUCET, CHERUIT, PAQUIN SOMETIMES. THE REST ARE HORRID.

THERE'S A BIG DIFFERENCE?

AN ENORMOUS ONE, MY LITTLE MAN.

OH! SORRY.

Exactly, without going so far as to say that the difference is as marked as between a statue from Reims Cathedral and one from the Saint-Augustin church.

OH, MENTIONING CATHEDRALS, I WAS TALKING TO YOU THE OTHER DAY ABOUT THE BALBEC CHURCH BEING LIKE A GREAT CLIFF, BUT ON THE OTHER HAND, LOOK AT THESE CLIFFS.

HERE'S A SKETCH DONE NEARBY AT CREUNIERS.

LOOK HOW THESE POWERFULLY, DELICATELY CUT OUT ROCKS MAKE YOU THINK OF A CATHEDRAL.

Albertine and Andrée were certain that I had to have gone there hundreds of times. If so, it was without knowing it, nor suspecting that one day the sight of them would inspire in me such a thirst for beauty.

There were days when we snacked in one of those farm-restaurants in the neighborhood. These farms were called Les Écorres, Marie-Thérèse, the Croix-d'Herland, the Bagatelle, the California, and the Marie-Antoinette.

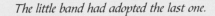

The little band had adopted the last one.

But sometimes, instead of going to a farm, we'd climb to the top of the cliff.

Between their faces close to one another, the air separating them traced out azure paths as though cleared out by a gardener who wanted to create a little space so he could move around all the different roses.

For the most part, the very faces of these girls were clouded with that muddled blush of the dawn from which their true traits had not yet emerged.

The moment comes so quickly when you no longer have anything to await, when your body is frozen in an immobility that holds no further surprises.

That radiant morning is so short that you start liking only the youngest girls.

It was with delight that I listened to their chirping.

Just like those children who possess a gland that helps them digest milk but which no longer exists in adults, there was in the twittering of these girls notes which women no longer possess.

Our provisions exhausted, we played games that had till then seemed boring to me.

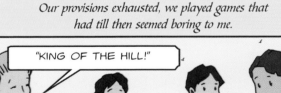

"KING OF THE HILL!"

NO! "WHO LAUGHS THE FIRST!"

It wasn't merely a social gathering or a walk with Mme. de Villeparisis that I'd have sacrificed to the "ferret" or "guessing games" of my friends. I also turned away other friends.

Whereas with Mme de Villeparisis or Saint-Loup I'd have shown by my words much more pleasure than I truly felt, on the contrary lying there amongst the girls, the plenitude I felt overwhelmed the scarceness and infrequency of our conversations, and overflowed with floods of happiness the lapping of which died away at the feet of these young roses.

One day…

WHO'S GOT A PENCIL?

Andrée supplied one, and Rosemonde the paper.

MY DEAR LITTLE WOMEN, I FORBID YOU TO GAZE UPON WHAT I'M WRITING.

MAKE SURE THEY DON'T SEE.

BUT INSTEAD OF WRITING SILLY STUFF,

I SHOULD SHOW YOU THE LETTER GISELE WROTE ME THIS MORNING.

Gisèle had thought she should send to her friend the composition she'd written for her diploma.

SUBJECT: "SOPHOCLES WRITES FROM HELL TO RACINE TO CONSOLE HIM OVER THE FAILURE OF ATHALIE."

I'LL HAVE MY ROMANCE WITH ALBERTINE.

One afternoon when we're playing the "Ferret"...

I was enviously watching Albertine's neighbor, a young man, telling myself that if I were in his spot, I'd be able to touch my friend's hands for minutes beyond hope that might perhaps never recur.

Already, just on its own, contact with Albertine's hands would have been a delight to me. Pressing Albertine's hand had a sensual sweetness. That pressure seemed to let you penetrate into the girl's being, into the depth of her senses, like the sound of her laugh, indecent in the manner of a cooing or certain animal cries.

I deliberately let myself grab the ring and once in the middle, when she went by, pretended to not notice it, and followed her with my eyes, awaiting the moment when it would arrive in the hands of Albertine's neighbor.

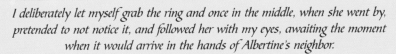

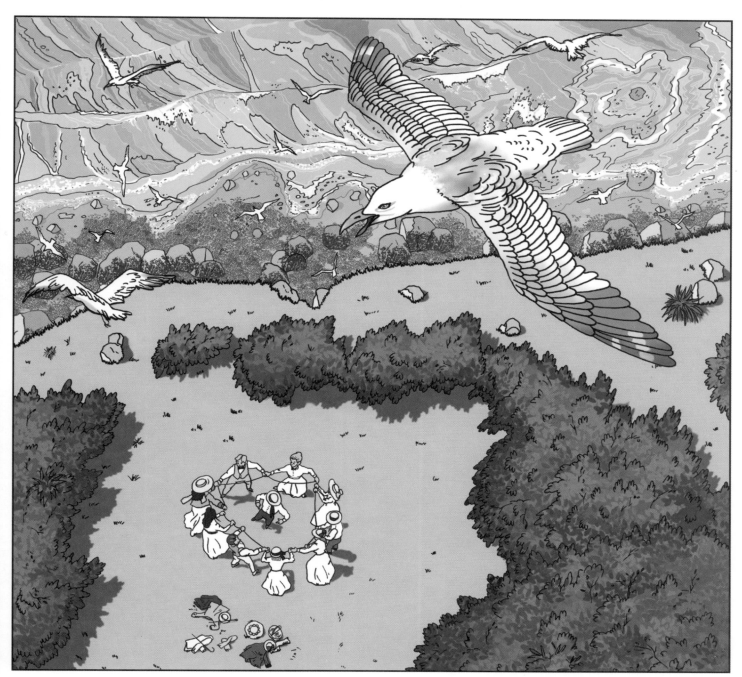

WE CERTAINLY ARE IN THE BEAUTIFUL GROVE...

"THE FERRET OF THE GROVE HAS PASSED THIS WAY, MILADIES; THE FERRET OF THE BEAUTIFUL GROVE PASSED BY THIS DAY "

YOU HAVE THE TRESSES OF LAURA DIANTI, OF ELEANOR OF GUYENNE, AND HER DESCENDANT SO BELOVED OF CHATEAUBRIAND.

YOU SHOULD ALWAYS WEAR YOUR HAIR A LITTLE DOWN.

The players became astonished at my stupidity for not catching the ring.

Suddenly the ring passed to Albertine's neighbor.

Immediately...

He was obliged to take my place in the middle of the circle, and I took his beside Albertine.

I felt the slight pressure of Albertine's hand against my own, and her caressing finger that was slipping beneath my finger,

SHE'S TAKING ADVANTAGE OF THE GAME TO SHOW ME THAT SHE LIKES ME.

....and I saw that, at the same time, she was giving me a wink that she was trying to keep hidden.

WELL, TAKE IT ALREADY, I'VE BEEN PASSING IT TO YOU FOR AN HOUR.

The ferret spied the ring,

and I had to return to the middle.

YOU CAN'T PLAY IF YOU DON'T WANT TO PAY ATTENTION AND MAKE OTHER PEOPLE LOSE.

WE WON'T INVITE HIM ANYMORE ON DAYS WHEN WE PLAY, ANDREE, OR I WON'T COME THEN.

Andrée tried to make light of Albertine's reproaches.

WE'RE VERY CLOSE TO THE CREUNIERS PLACE YOU SO WANTED TO SEE.

HEY, I'LL TAKE YOU THERE BY A PRETTY, LITTLE PATH WHILE THESE SILLY THINGS ACT LIKE EIGHT-YEAR-OLDS.

As Andrée was extremely kind to me, en route I told her everything about Albertine that seemed likely to make me appeal to her.

Andrée told me she was very fond of her, too; yet my compliments with respect to her friend didn't seem to please her.

Suddenly…

?

I stopped, touched to the heart by a sweet, childhood memory.

I'd just recognized a hawthorn bush, flowerless, alas, since spring's end.

Around me was floating an atmosphere of the old month of Mary, of Sunday afternoons.

Andrée, with a charming divination, let me chat for a moment with the bush's leaves.

I rejoined Andree and again began to sing Albertine's praises to her.

It seemed impossible to me that she wouldn't repeat to Albertine what I'd said.

And yet I've never heard that Albertine learned of it.

Listening to the charming things she was telling me about a possible affection between Albertine and me, it seemed that she'd be determined to work with all her might to make it come about.

Of the thousand refinements of kindness that Andrée had, Albertine would have been incapable, and yet I wasn't certain of the profound goodness of the former like I would later be of the latter.

SO, HERE ARE YOUR FAMOUS CREUNIERS,

AND YOU'RE LUCKY, TOO, IN THE SAME WEATHER AND SAME LIGHT AS WHEN ELSTIR PAINTED THEM.

But I was still too sad at having fallen, during the "ferret" game, from such a pinnacle of hope.

Several days after the game of "ferret," having let ourselves stray too far on a walk, we were very fortunate to find two small, two-seater "tubs."

ROSEMONDE COULD COME WITH ME

OR ANDREE PERHAPS...

I led everyone to decide, as though against my will, that I should take Albertine with me, to whose company I pretended to resign myself for good or ill.

The following week, I scarcely attempted to see Albertine. I pretended to prefer Andrée.

Whenever I spoke with Andrée of Albertine, I affected a coldness by which Andrée was perhaps less duped than I by its apparent credulity.

I KNOW WELL ENOUGH THAT YOU LOVE ALBERTINE AND THAT YOU'RE DOING EVERYTHING POSSIBLE TO GET CLOSER TO HER FAMILY.

42

About a month after the day when we'd played "ferret"...

ALBERTINE HAS TO GO SPEND TWO DAYS AT HER AUNT'S, MADAME DE BONTEMPS; I HEARD THAT SINCE SHE'D HAVE TO TAKE THE EARLY TRAIN, SHE'D BE SPENDING THE NIGHT BEFORE AT THE GRAND-HOTEL.

I DON'T BELIEVE IT ONE BIT.

MOREOVER IT WON'T GET YOU ANYWHERE AT ALL, FOR I'M QUITE CERTAIN THAT ALBERTINE WON'T WANT TO SEE YOU, IF SHE COMES TO THE HOTEL ALONE.

IT WOULDN'T BE PROPER.

AND JUST WHY DO YOU FIGURE IT'D MATTER TO ME WHETHER YOU SEE HER OR NOT?

I REALLY DON'T CARE.

We were joined by Octave...

then by Albertine...

IT SEEMS THAT MADAME DE VILLEPARISIS HAS MADE A REQUEST TO YOUR FATHER THAT DIABOLO NOT BE PLAYED ON THE BEACH WALK ANY LONGER;

SHE GOT HIT IN THE FACE BY A BALL.

YEAH. IT'S RIDICULOUS. THERE'S ALREADY NOT MUCH FUN TO BE HAD HERE.

I DON'T SEE WHY THAT LADY WOULD MAKE SUCH A BIG DEAL ABOUT IT, OLD MME. DE CAMBREMER GOT HIT, TOO, AND SHE DIDN'T COMPLAIN.

He left us, as did Andrée. I remained alone with Albertine.

DO YOU SEE THAT NOW I'M WEARING MY HAIR THE WAY YOU LIKE. JUST LOOK AT MY TRESS. NOBODY KNOWS WHOM I'M DOING IT FOR. MY AUNT WILL MAKE FUN OF ME, TOO. I WON'T TELL HER WHY EITHER.

I asked her if the rumors of her plans were true.

YES, I'M SPENDING TONIGHT AT YOUR HOTEL AND SINCE I'VE GOT A BIT OF A COLD, I'LL GO TO BED BEFORE DINNER. YOU COULD SIT BESIDE MY BED WHILE I EAT AND AFTERWARDS WE'LL PLAY WHATEVER YOU LIKE.

COME EARLY,

SO WE'LL HAVE LOTS OF TIME TO OURSELVES.

I went to dine with my grandmother. I felt within myself a secret of which she was unaware.

What was to happen soon, I wasn't very sure of.

In any case, the Grand Hotel and the evening no longer seemed empty to me; they contained my happiness.

Those few steps from the landing to Albertine's room, those few steps that no one could any longer prevent, I took them with delight, with prudence.

Then suddenly, I thought that I was wrong to have any doubts; she'd told me to come while she was in bed.

Her cheek was traversed from top to bottom by one of her long, dark, curling tresses, which she'd let down entirely to please me.

?

I was going to savor the odor, the taste held by this unknown rosy fruit.

Seeing me throw myself upon her to kiss her...

STOP OR I'LL RING!

But I told myself that a girl didn't have a young man come secretly for no reason.

GLING!

?

Albertine had rung with all her might.

44

Upon her return from her aunt's a week later:

I FORGIVE YOU. I'M EVEN SORRY FOR HAVING CAUSED YOU ANY PAIN, BUT DON'T EVER TRY THAT AGAIN.

My dreams abandoned her once they ceased to be nourished by the hope of a possession of which I'd believed them to be independent. From then on, they found themselves free to transfer themselves to this or that friend of Albertine's.

She was certainly sorry for not having been able to make me happy and gave me a small, gold pencil.

YOU'RE DOING ME A GREAT PLEASURE, LESS GREAT HOWEVER THAN THE ONE I'D HAVE HAD IF YOU'D LET ME KISS YOU.

....IT WOULD HAVE MADE ME SO HAPPY; HOW COULD IT HAVE HURT YOU? I'M SURPRISED YOU WOULDN'T LET ME.

I'M WONDERING WHAT SORTS OF GIRLS YOU COULD HAVE MET FOR MY BEHAVIOR TO HAVE SURPRISED YOU.

MY OPINION IS THAT THESE ARE THINGS OF NO IMPORTANCE...

....LETTING YOURSELF BE KISSED, AND EVEN MORE, BY A FRIEND, SINCE YOU SAY THAT I'M YOUR FRIEND...

YOU ARE, BUT I'VE HAD OTHERS BEFORE YOU.

WELL, THERE'S NOT A ONE OF THEM WHO'D HAVE TRIED SOMETHING LIKE THAT.

THEY KNEW THE TWO SMACKS THEY'D HAVE GOTTEN.

BUT I'M SURE THAT YOU DON'T REALLY CARE FOR ME. ADMIT THAT IT'S ANDREE WHOM YOU PREFER.

AND YOU'RE QUITE RIGHT; SHE'S A LOT NICER THAN I AM AND SHE'S BEAUTIFUL!

OH! YOU MEN!

For all the long hours I'd spent chatting, eating, playing with these girls, I didn't even remember

that they were the same ruthless, sensual virgins I'd seen, like in a fresco, parading alongside the sea.

And, after all, getting close enough to things and people that, from afar, had seemed beautiful and mysterious to make us realize that they're without mystery and beauty is as good a way as any of solving the problem of existence;

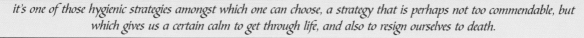

it's one of those hygienic strategies amongst which one can choose, a strategy that is perhaps not too commendable, but which gives us a certain calm to get through life, and also to resign ourselves to death.

Albertine left first, abruptly.

SHE DIDN'T SAY WHY OR WHATEVER AND THEN SHE LEFT.

My girl friends left Balbec, not all at once, but within the same week.

The local train, which no longer had enough passengers, discontinued its service until the following spring.

WHAT WE LACK HERE ARE THE MEANS OF COMMOTION.

I WASN'T ADEQUATELY SUPPORTED.

YOU'LL SEE NEXT YEAR WHAT A PHALANX I'LL BRING TOGETHER.

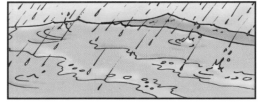

Sometimes, the driving rain confined my grandmother and me, with the Casino being closed, to almost completely deserted rooms, as in the bottom of a ship's hold when the wind is in a gale.

The chief magistrate from Caen, the head of the Bar in Cherbourg, an American woman and her daughters, came up to us, started conversations, invented some way to make the hours less long, revealed a talent…

46

All in all, I'd not really taken advantage of Balbec, which only strengthened my desire to return there.

NEXT YEAR, I'LL RESERVE BETTER ROOMS FOR YOU.

But I was now attached to mine where I'd enter no longer noticing the fragrance of the vetiver.

We finally had to leave Balbec, the cold and damp having become too penetrating. I forgot almost immediately those last weeks.

What I would recall almost invariably whenever I thought about Balbec were those moments when every morning during the nice weather, since I was to go out every afternoon with Albertine and her friends, my grandmother, on the doctor's orders, made me stay in bed in the darkness.

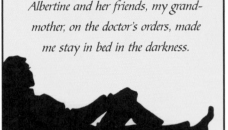

I knew that my friends were on the walkway, but I didn't see them. I guessed their presence; I'd hear their laughter muted like that of the Nereids in the soft lapping that reached my ears.

I kept the great, violet curtains closed. But, despite the pins with which Françoise attached them, despite the fabrics taken from here and there that she added to them, the darkness wasn't complete.

WE LOOKED TO SEE IF YOU'D COME DOWN. BUT YOUR SHUTTERS WERE STILL CLOSED EVEN WHEN TIME FOR THE CONCERT.

Noon would sound; Françoise would finally arrive.

The summer day that she revealed seemed as dead, as immemorial as a sumptuous, millennial mummy that our old servant had, only as a precaution, unwound from all its linens, before displaying it, embalmed in its golden robe.

FIN